Collaboration and Propensities

Nadja Quante

Sound plays an important role in Jimmy Robert's work, not as his own form of expression – Robert is not a musician – but rather, as a resonating space. The artist record *Call and Response* by Robert thus brings together pieces created in connection with performances and exhibitions by the artist. These pieces provide insights into his collaborative practice in conjunction with his performances.

The record is released following the exhibition *la musique dans la chambre*, which took place in the spring of 2022 at Künstlerhaus Bremen. The exhibition addressed the question of how Robert's performance works can continue to be shown apart from being performed again in exhibitions: How can one approach a performance work anew without re-staging it? Starting from this question, the exhibition focused particularly on sound and brought together videos, works on paper, as well as sculptural elements and sound created in the framework of his performances. The record *Call and Response* expands the exhibition and gathers sound pieces produced by Robert as well as by other artists – often in connection with Robert's works:

European Portraits is a performance and installation that Robert first presented at PEER Gallery in London in 2017. The work was created in response to the Brexit vote and highlights some of the complex personal and political consequences of that event. For the work, Robert – who himself lived in the United Kingdom for several years – composed poetic text portraits of eight different individuals.

The first of the eight texts, titled *L* (on side A1), is heard on the record and read by the artist himself.

The same text forms the basis for the sound on *European Portraits* (A3), by composer, artist, and DJ Ain Bailey, who Robert has collaborated with on four performances. Bailey's composition for *European Portraits* is based on Bailey's own voice recording of a text portrait. What is heard, however, are not the words but the moments of breathing and silence between the words. In the performance, live sound and recording were overlaid and arranged in a call-and-response manner often used in the West Indian tradition by dancers and drummers in dialogue.

Descendances du nu is a body of work created in 2016 in the context of a performance and site-specific installation at the Synagogue de Delme in France. The work is strongly influenced by the architecture of the performance venue: a former synagogue that is now used as an exhibition space. The sound work for *Descendances du nu* (A2), also composed by Bailey, gives space to voices that were absent and spatially separated in the previous use of the building as synagogue. These are the female voices of the employees who worked in or near the institution at the time of Robert's exhibition.

Emma Hedditch's piece *Many* (A4) was created as a soundtrack for Robert's video performance *Saynètes* (2004). The artist and musician is a long-time friend of Robert's, with whom he collaborated

Sound spielt eine wichtige Rolle in Jimmy Roberts Werk. Nicht als seine eigene Ausdrucksform – Robert selbst ist kein Musiker –, sondern eher als Resonanzraum. Roberts Künstlerschallplatte *Call and Response* bringt Stücke zusammen, die im Rahmen von Performances und Ausstellungen des Künstlers entstanden sind. Die Stücke geben Einblicke in Roberts kollaborative Praxis in Verbindung mit seinen Performances.

Die Schallplatte erscheint in Anschluss an die Ausstellung *la musique dans la chambre*, die im Frühjahr 2022 im Künstlerhaus Bremen stattgefunden hat. Die Ausstellung ging der Frage nach, wie Roberts Performancearbeiten abseits von Wiederaufführungen in Ausstellungen weiter gezeigt werden können. Wie kann man sich einer Performancearbeit neu nähern, ohne sie zu reinszenieren? Ausgehend von dieser Frage legte die Ausstellung einen besonderen Schwerpunkt auf den Klang und versammelte Videos, Papierarbeiten, skulpturale Elemente und Sound, die im Rahmen seiner Performances entstanden sind. Die Platte *Call and Response* erweitert die Ausstellung und versammelt Tonstücke, die von Robert und anderen Künstler:innen – meist in Verbindung mit Roberts Werken – produziert wurden.

European Portraits ist eine Performance und Installation, die Robert erstmals 2017 in der PEER Gallery in London präsentiert hat. Die Arbeit ist in Reaktion auf das Brexit-Votum entstanden und beleuchtet einige der komplexen persönlichen und politischen Folgen dieses Ereignisses. Für die Arbeit verfasste Robert – der selbst mehrere Jahre in Großbritannien gelebt hat – poetische Porträts von acht verschiedenen Individuen.

Der erste der acht Texte, mit dem Titel *L* (A1), ist auf der Platte vom Künstler selbst eingesprochen zu hören.

Derselbe Text bildet auch die Grundlage für den Sound zu *European Portraits* (A3), den die Komponistin, Künstlerin und DJ Ain Bailey komponiert hat. Mit Bailey hat Robert bereits für vier Performances kollaboriert. Baileys Komposition für *European Portraits* basiert auf Baileys eigener Stimmaufnahme eines der Textporträts. Was jedoch zu hören ist, sind nicht die Worte, sondern die Momente des Atmens und der Stille zwischen den Worten. In der Performance wurden Live-Sound und Aufnahme in einer Art Call-and-Response überlagert und arrangiert, das häufig in der westindischen Tradition von Tanz und Trommel im Dialog verwendet wird.

Descendances du nu ist ein Werkkomplex, der 2016 im Kontext einer Performance und ortsspezifischen Installation in der Synagogue de Delme in Frankreich entstanden ist. Die Arbeit ist stark von der Architektur des Aufführungsortes beeinflusst: einer ehemaligen Synagoge, die heute als Ausstellungsraum genutzt wird. Die Soundarbeit zu *Descendances du nu* (A2), die ebenfalls Bailey komponiert hat, gibt den Stimmen Raum, die in der vorherigen Nutzung des Gebäudes als Synagoge abwesend und räumlich separiert waren. Es sind die weiblichen Stimmen der Mitarbeiterinnen, die zum Zeitpunkt von Roberts Ausstellung in der Institution oder deren Nachbarschaft arbeiteten.

Emma Hedditchs Stück *Many* (A4) ist als Soundtrack für Roberts Videoperformance *Saynètes* (2004) entstanden. Die Künstlerin und Musikerin ist eine langjährige Freundin von Robert, mit der er bereits

in various film and video contexts while studying at Goldsmiths College in London.

The electronic track for Robert's performance *Abolibibelo* (B1) was again composed by Bailey. The performance was created in 2015 for the retrospective of Bauhaus artist and theater designer Xanti Schawinsky at the Migros Museum in Zurich. In the performance, in which Robert appears in a costume made of white paper strips, the artist plays with the viewers' expectations and blurs the boundaries between the "modern" and the "primitive." At the end of the performance, Robert reads a Dadaist text, which is the first piece heard on the second side of the record.

Technique et Sentiment VI (B3) is a soundscape and sound document of a non-public performance Robert recorded in the summer of 2021 in the white cube of Tanya Leighton Gallery in Berlin, who represents the artist's work. In the recording, a series of different movements can be heard in the space: something is dragged across the floor, something falls. It is the artist handling a long roll of paper, rolling it up, walking over it, dancing with it. With the movements, his breath becomes stronger and stronger. The presence of the body manifests itself in the sounds triggered by its forces and limits. The artist's body is brought into space without actually being present. Robert plays with the presences and absences of the studio and gallery spaces. He refers to this work as non-performance: How can one refer to performance without performing it?

Plié (B4) is a text by Robert that was performed in the context of a performance at the Leopold-Hoesch-Museum in Düren, 2020, by vocalist Ina Hagenau, who paced through the empty museum spaces while singing. Originally planned as a public live event, the pandemic changed it to a performance that echoed off walls without an audience.

Wanna talk about reading? (B5) was created in 2017 in the context of Robert's homonymous exhibition at Western Front in Vancouver, Canada. For the performance, Robert collaborated with dancer, teacher, and artist Jane Ellison, whose studio was adjacent to Western Front's exhibition space. Without ever meeting in person, Ellison and Robert engaged in a conversation. For this, Robert prepared a set of specific questions that Ellison answered in her recordings. She shared thoughts about her personal history, as well as about visualization, learning, or embodiment. The questions related to a possible physical collaboration between Robert and Ellison that in the end never took place. However, these voice recordings formed the basis for Robert's performance, whose movements responded to Ellison's words, the cadence of her voice, as well as objects and images in the space. In the excerpt, *Visualizing*, Ellison talks about the connections between visualizations and movements in the context of her teaching.

Draw the Line (B6) is a recording of Robert writing the text *Draw the Line* in which he relates to American artist Carolee Schneemann's performance *Up To and Including Her Limits* (1976). In her performance, Schneemann lowered herself with a rope over a large canvas while holding pencils in her hand. Extending her arms, she marked the surface around and below her. Through the act of writing the text, using

während seines Studiums am Goldsmiths College in London in verschiedenen Film- und Videokontexten kollaboriert hat.

Der elektronische Track für Roberts Performance *Abolibibelo* (B1) wurde wiederum von Bailey komponiert. Die Performance entstand 2015 für die Retrospektive des Bauhaus-Künstlers und Theaterdesigners Xanti Schawinsky im Migros Museum in Zürich. In der Performance, in der Robert in einem Kostüm aus weißen Papierstreifen auftritt, spielt der Künstler mit den Erwartungen der Betrachter:innen und verwischte die Grenzen zwischen dem „Modernen" und dem „Primitiven". Am Ende der Performance liest Robert einen dadaistischen Text, der als erstes Stück auf der zweiten Seite der Platte zu hören ist.

Technique et Sentiment VI (B3) ist eine Soundscape und das Klangdokument einer nicht-öffentlichen Performance, die Robert im Sommer 2021 im White Cube der Galerie Tanya Leighton in Berlin, die ihn vertritt, aufgenommen hat. Auf der Aufnahme sind eine Reihe unterschiedlicher Bewegungen im Raum zu hören: Etwas wird über den Boden gezogen, etwas fällt. Es ist der Künstler, der mit einer langen Rolle Papier hantiert, sie aufrollt, über sie geht, mit ihr tanzt. Mit den Bewegungen wird sein Atem immer stärker. Die Anwesenheit des Körpers manifestiert sich in den Geräuschen, die durch seine Kräfte und Grenzen ausgelöst werden. Der Körper des Künstlers wird in den Raum gebracht, ohne tatsächlich präsent zu sein. Robert spielt mit den An- und Abwesenheiten der Studio- und Galerieräume. Er bezeichnet diese Arbeit als Non-Performance: Wie kann man auf eine Performance verweisen, ohne sie aufzuführen?

Bei *Plié* (B4) handelt es sich um einen Text von Robert, der im Kontext einer Performance im Leopold-Hoesch-Museum in Düren, 2020, von der singend durch die leeren Ausstellungsräume schreitenden Vokalistin Ina Hagenau interpretiert wurde. Ursprünglich als öffentliche Live-Veranstaltung geplant, wurde *Plié* durch die Corona-Pandemie zu einer Performance, die von Wänden ohne Publikum widerhallte.

Wanna talk about reading? (B5) entstand 2017 im Kontext von Roberts gleichnamiger Ausstellung im von Künstler:innen geführten Zentrum Western Front in Vancouver, Kanada. Robert kollaborierte für die Performance mit der Tänzerin, Lehrerin und Künstlerin Jane Ellison, deren Atelier an den Ausstellungsraum von Western Front angrenzt. Ohne sich jemals persönlich zu treffen, führten Ellison und Robert eine Konversation. Robert bereitete dafür eine Reihe spezifischer Fragen vor, die Ellison in Sprachaufnahmen beantwortete. Ellison teilt darin ihre Gedanken über ihre persönliche Geschichte, aber auch Visualisierung, Lernen oder Verkörperung. Die Fragen bezogen sich auf eine mögliche physische Zusammenarbeit zwischen Robert und Ellison, die letztendlich nie zustande kam. Jedoch bildeten die Sprachaufnahmen die Grundlage für Roberts Performance, der mit seinen Bewegungen auf Ellisons Worte, die Kadenz ihrer Stimme sowie Objekte und Bilder im Raum reagierte. In dem Auszug *Visualizing* erzählt Ellison von den Zusammenhängen von Visualisierungen und Bewegungen im Rahmen ihrer Lehre.

Draw the Line (B6) ist eine Aufnahme davon, wie Robert den Text *Draw the Line* schreibt, in dem er sich auf die Performance *Up To and Including Her Limits* (1976) der amerikanischen Künstlerin Carolee

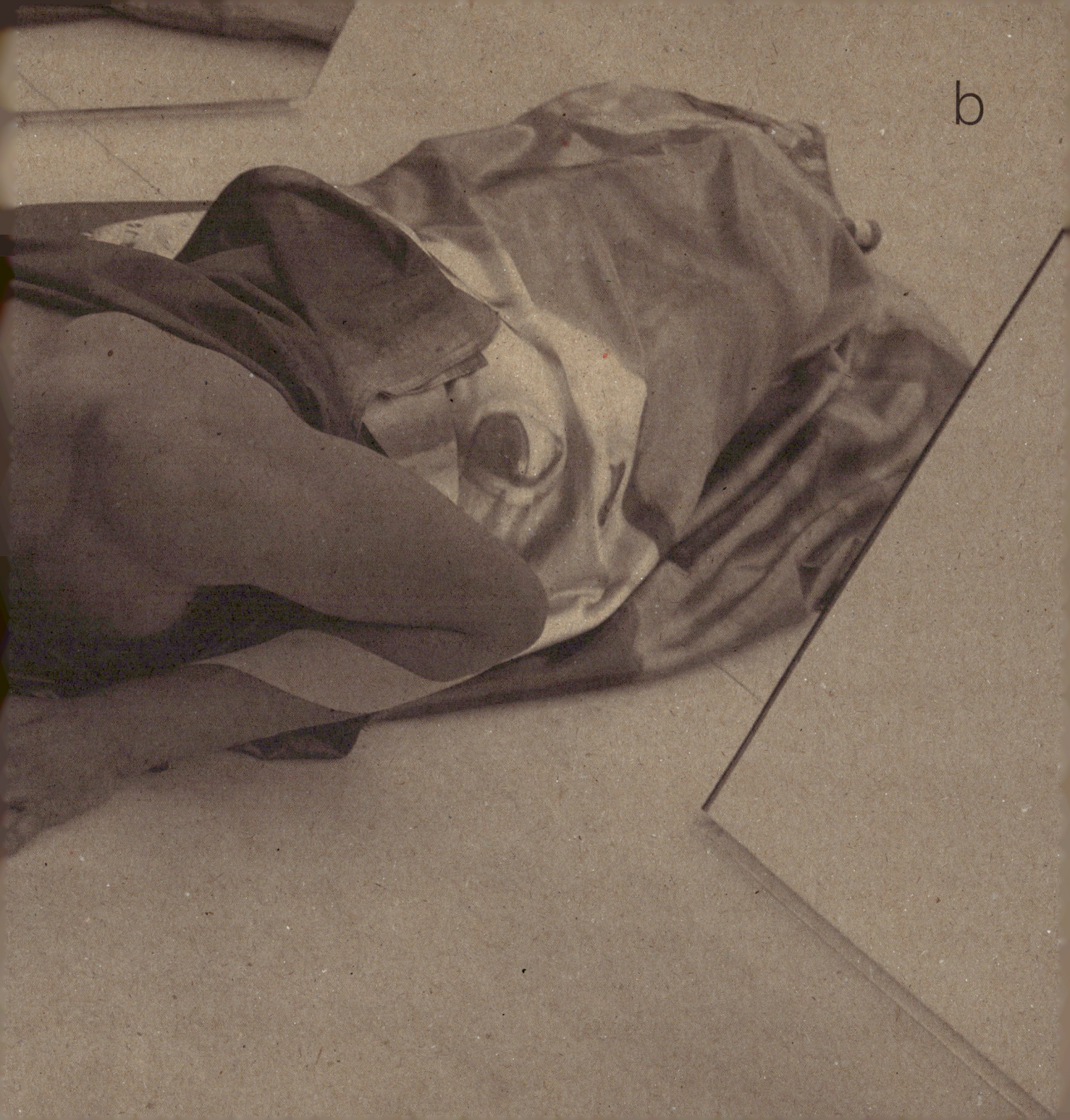

b

a pencil on paper, Robert builds a connection
with her and her performance.

The last track on the record, *Amorijisa* (B7), is an
excerpt from a piece Robert recorded with artist
Rosa Barba in 2005. Robert reads a text from
Marguerite Duras's *Hiroshima mon amour* (1960)
over the rhythmic melody of Barba's sounds.

The sounds gathered on this record make Robert's
performances as well as their spaces and contexts
reverberate: the architecture of the synagogue
or the presentational context of the museum, the
exhibition space in the context of a studio building,
the political space of the United Kingdom, or
the gallery. The pieces echo these spaces. They
comprise a wide spectrum of sounds – between
spoken word, sounding text, melodic soundtrack,
and droning composition. What unites them
is a great trust in collaboration and a generosity
of the artist to give space to resonance.

Schneemann bezieht. In ihrer Performance ließ sich Schneemann mit Bleistiften in der Hand an einem Seil über eine große Leinwand herab. Mit ausgestreckten Armen markierte sie die Fläche um sich herum und unter ihr. Durch den Akt des Schreibens des Texts mit einem Bleistift auf Papier stellt Robert eine Verbindung zu ihr und ihrer Performance her.

Der letzte Track der Platte, *Amorijisa* (B7), ist ein Auszug aus einem Stück, das Robert 2005 gemeinsam mit der Künstlerin Rosa Barba aufgenommen hat. Robert liest einen Text aus Marguerite Duras' *Hiroshima mon amour* (1960) über die rhythmische Melodie von Barbas Klängen.

Die auf dieser Platte versammelten Sounds lassen Roberts Performances sowie ihre Räume und Kontexte nachhallen: die Architektur der Synagoge oder den Präsentationszusammenhang des Museums, den Ausstellungsraum im Ateliergebäude, den politischen Raum Großbritanniens oder die Galerie. Die Stücke spiegeln diese Räume wider. Sie umfassen ein breites Spektrum von Klängen – zwischen gesprochenem Wort, klingendem Text, melodischem Soundtrack und dröhnender Komposition. Was sie eint, ist das große Vertrauen in die Zusammenarbeit und die Großzügigkeit des Künstlers, der Resonanz Raum zu geben.

C

d

static shots and elevations

Boogie Intimacy

Mason Leaver-Yap

Reading other people's texts aloud feels good. Having someone else's thoughts jangle around in another mouth, hearing it come out at a different speed – the weight of another tongue leans more heavily or lingers on a word longer than was initially intended, accented anew. Our mouths needn't know how to spell, just how to move breath through lips – "L," "Elle," "El."

Ritual languages (like prayers, like songs) know the pleasure of this collaboration and flauntingly desire to mingle their words with our histories and bodies, blending their older fragments with oral selves to achieve dissemination, circulation, transmission. The rhyme seeks out its memorialization because it wants to ignite repetition, find willing hosts to replicate its structure. And yet, we're never quite faithful to the original. We always repeat, rehearse, realize inside our own attitudes, gestures, breathing patterns. This is how influence flows through us, connects us impossibly with past incantations. In our desires to be with the old language, we transform it, maybe even disfiguring it in our remembering and working through our imprecisions as an act of additive creation.

(Anne Carson translates Sappho's fragments: "someone will remember us / I say / even in another time". I hear the desire and pride in her words, as well as the doubtfulness and desperation in the pauses. Both can be true. Repeat after me, the poet says, hoping for an echo, waiting inside the gaps.)

While working together on their performance in a basement speakeasy in Berlin, my friend Evan sends me Jean Fisher's essay "Reflections on Echo." I read it through what we are doing together and write some notes to send Evan: "A by-product of sound and thus of being present (or having been present), the echo is the formal repetition of content. It is a rhythm in spatial and sonorous entanglement with time. Once embodied and now disembodied, it becomes the structural relay between transmitters and receivers, speakers and listeners. Even a silence repeated is still an echo of things unspoken."

Over a year later, I'm in the same basement, working on another performance – this time with Jimmy. We're listening to a recording of Ian reading aloud Jessica Mitford's essay "Behind the Formaldehyde Curtain" from her 1963 book *The American Way of Death*. Ian recorded it for Jimmy on a CD-R as a text to share and discuss. In the gaps between Ian's clipped accent, street sounds leak into the background. Perhaps it's the tone of his voice, but the recording has a slight metallic ring to it, a clatter. Jimmy and I speculate if it was recorded in a kitchen with the windows open. At the end, I hear the mic capturing the echoey click of Ian's mouse as he presses stop.

Jimmy wants to play this CD at the beginning of the performance and for the bar to feel a bit like a sex club. He suggests we replace the lighting with

Die Texte anderer Leute laut zu lesen, fühlt sich gut an. Die Gedanken einer Person in einem fremden Mund herumschwirren zu lassen, zu hören, wie sie in einer anderen Geschwindigkeit herauskommen – das Gewicht einer anderen Zunge lastet schwerer oder verweilt länger auf einem Wort als eigentlich beabsichtigt, setzt den Akzent neu. Unsere Münder müssen nicht wissen, wie man buchstabiert, sondern nur, wie man den Atem durch die Lippen schiebt – „L", „Elle", „El".

Rituelle Sprachen (wie Gebete, wie Lieder) kennen die Vorzüge dieser Zusammenkunft, sie streben nach einer Vermischung ihrer Worte mit unseren Geschichten (*histories*) und Körpern, indem sie vergangene Sprachfragmente mit einem oralen Ich vermengen. Auf diesem Weg entstehen Verbreitung, Zirkulation und Übertragung. Der Reim sucht sich sein Denkmal, denn er strebt nach Wiederholung, will willige Wirte finden, die seine Struktur nachbilden. Und doch sind wir dem Original nie ganz treu. Wir wiederholen, proben, erkennen immer wieder unsere eigenen Haltungen, Gesten, Atemmuster. So durchströmen uns Einflüsse, die uns unausweichlich mit vergangenen Beschwörungsformeln verbinden. In unserem Wunsch, mit der alten Sprache zu leben, verwandeln wir sie, verunstalten sie durch unsere Erinnerung und arbeiten uns durch die eigenen Ungenauigkeiten hindurch in einen Akt additiver Schaffensweise.

(Anne Carson übersetzt Sapphos Fragmente: „Someone will remember us / I say / even in another time." Ich höre in ihren Worten den Wunsch und den Stolz, aber auch die Zweifel und die Verzweiflung in den Pausen. Beides kann wahr sein. Sprich mir nach, sagt die Dichterin, in der Hoffnung auf ein Echo, das in den Lücken lauert.)

Mein/e Freund:in Evan schickt mir während unserer gemeinsamen Arbeit an einer Performance in einer Berliner Kellerkneipe Jean Fishers Essay „Reflections on Echo". Ich lese ihn und mache ein paar Notizen, die ich Evan schicke: „Das Echo ist ein Nebenprodukt des Klangs und damit der Anwesenheit (oder der gewesenen Anwesenheit) und die formale Wiederholung des Inhalts. Ein Rhythmus in räumlicher und klanglicher Verflechtung mit der Zeit. Einst verkörpert und nun entkörperlicht, wird es zum strukturgebenden Relais zwischen Sender:innen und Empfänger:innen, Sprecher:innen und Zuhörer:innen. Selbst ein wiederholtes Schweigen ist ein Echo des Unausgesprochenen."

Über ein Jahr später befinde ich mich im selben Keller und arbeite an einer weiteren Performance, diesmal mit Jimmy. Wir hören uns eine Aufnahme an, auf der Ian Jessica Mitfords Essay „Behind the Formaldehyde Curtain" aus ihrem 1963 erschienenen Buch *The American Way of Death* laut vorliest. Ian hat ihn, um ihn mit Jimmy zu teilen und zu diskutieren, auf eine CD-R aufgenommen. In die Pausen zwischen Ians abgehackten Betonungen dringen Straßengeräusche aus dem Hintergrund. Die Aufnahme hat einen leicht metallischen Klang, ein Klappern, möglicherweise der Unterton seiner Stimme. Jimmy und ich spekulieren, ob die Aufnahme in einer Küche mit offenen Fenstern gemacht wurde. Am Ende höre ich, wie das Mikrofon das echoartige Klicken von Ians Maus aufzeichnet, als er auf Stopp drückt.

Jimmy möchte die CD am Anfang der Performance abspielen, um der Bar den Anschein eines Sexclubs zu verleihen. Er schlägt vor, die Beleuchtung durch

red bulbs and pour out bottles of poppers onto the concrete floor. On opening night, I overcompensate by pouring too much and too early. I forget the public still need time to descend the staircase from the courtyard into the basement, and so the two invigilators and I linger in a large puddle of amyl nitrate, waiting at the bottom, warmly swaying. My flatmate Jim says the funk of leather cleaner has a whiff of the morgue. He talks about looking up from the ground and seeing the public gathered in the dark cellar, dim faces in a crypt. Everyone silent, listening, inhaling one another's moisture – the poppers evaporating with body warmth, the audience making the performance for each other.

At the end of Ian's reading, Jimmy wants the public to be released into the main hall upstairs, bathed in white light turning to dark blue. There's something alarming about that color transition. I think of the brightness of teeth and dandruff on a black-light dance floor, as well as the UV lights in inner-city bus stations that I grew up around in the 1990s – lit so no one could find a vein. (How horrific, to invent a light that intentionally sends vulnerable people into the dark.) But the blue in the hall is thicker – more bruised – and softened by a smoke machine saturating the hall with the appearance of a secret. Gathering clouds hiss along to Ain's throbbing remix of Diana Ross's *Love Hangover*, and these two textures lean into the congregation of soft bodies, the fog reducing everyone to apparitions – a group disassembling. The smoke disperses, and Jimmy reappears lighting a fag, casually reciting Grace Jones dead pan – summoning her as icon, as blue-black in black on brown, as *Nightclubbing* in 1981.

(John Berger affectionately describes the time of a cigarette as a parenthesis: "If it is shared you are both in that parenthesis. It's like a proscenium arch for a dialogue." Jimmy calls it a pause: "But people are paying attention because of the gesture. I mean, it's smoke, it's literally nothing. But you put it under a light, and it appears.")

F.

Boogie intimacy. That's what Douglas Crimp calls the moment when you're on the dancefloor with a stranger. "It's not a couples thing," he stresses, this "in-the-moment union for sharing pleasure" – looking, inviting, mirroring, curiously performing for one another, spontaneously figuring out how bodies might fit together for the duration of a song or a whole night. Crimp believed boogie intimacy lasted well beyond lights-up, though; it was a radical forerunner of gay liberation, "the expansion of affectional possibility." I don't want to theorize the fun out of the dancefloor as if I'm wringing sweat out of an otherwise juicy shirt, but I appreciate how the willingness to invent sensual collaborations can be a rehearsal for other shared actions – for solidarity and experimentation in different environments.

Jimmy, Ain, and Em are remembering all the nightclubs they used to meet at, how their friendship came through the occupation of and participation in these spaces. There's a pointed nostalgia in this conversation taking place in a moment where there are no nightclubs, just lockdowns. Em describes how organizing clubs can serve as on-ramps to developing and participating in mutual aid structures: both share similar skills dedicated to creating relations that produce physical and emotional spaces for self-organized actions. Both are refusals of isolation. Em mentions a

rote Glühbirnen zu ersetzen und Poppers-Flaschen auf dem Betonboden auszuschütten. Am Eröffnungsabend übertreibe ich und schütte zu viel und zu früh aus. Ich vergesse, dass das Publikum noch Zeit braucht, um die Treppe vom Innenhof in den Keller hinunterzusteigen, und so stehen die beiden Aufsichtspersonen und ich uns warm schunkelnd unten in einer großen Pfütze aus Amylnitrat und warten. Mein Mitbewohner Jim sagt, der Geruch von Lederreiniger habe einen Hauch von Leichenschauhaus. Er erzählt, wie er vom Fußboden aufschaute und die Leute im dunklen Keller versammelt sah, schemenhafte Gesichter in einer Gruft. Alle schweigen, hören zu, atmen den Dunst des anderen ein – die Wärme der Körper lässt die Poppers verdampfen, das Publikum performt füreinander.

Am Ende von Ians Lesung möchte Jimmy, dass das Publikum in die Haupthalle im Obergeschoss hinaufgeht. Sie ist in weißes Licht getaucht, das in ein dunkles Blau übergeht. Dieser Farbübergang hat etwas Beunruhigendes an sich. Ich denke an die strahlenden Zähne und Schuppen auf einer Tanzfläche mit Schwarzlicht und an die UV-Lichter in innerstädtischen Busbahnhöfen, in der Gegend, in der ich in den 1990er-Jahren aufgewachsen bin – so beleuchtet, dass die Adern nicht zu finden sind. (Wie furchtbar, ein Licht zu entwickeln, das schutzlose Menschen absichtlich in die Dunkelheit schickt.) Aber das Blau in der Halle ist satter – gequetscht; es wird durch eine Nebelmaschine gedämpft, die die Halle wie ein Geheimnis erscheinen lässt. Die aufsteigenden Wolken fauchen zu Ains hämmerndem Remix von Diana Ross' *Love Hangover*, die Texturen schmiegen sich an die Versammlung weicher Körper, der Nebel macht alle zu geisterhaften Erscheinungen – eine Gruppe,

die sich aufgelöst hat. Der Rauch verzieht sich, und Jimmy taucht wieder auf, zündet sich eine Kippe an und rezitiert beiläufig Grace Jones, beschwört sie herauf als Ikone, als Blauschwarz in Schwarz auf Braun, als *Nightclubbing* von 1981.

(John Berger beschreibt die Zigarettenzeit liebevoll als Klammer: „Wenn sie geteilt wird, befinden sich beide in dieser Klammer. Es ist wie ein Proszeniumsbogen für einen Dialog." Jimmy nennt es eine Pause: „Aber durch die Geste werden die Leute aufmerksam. Ich meine, es ist Rauch, es ist im Grunde nichts. Aber wenn man ihn gegen das Licht hält, wird er sichtbar.")

◢

Boogie intimacy, so nennt Douglas Crimp den Moment, wenn man mit einem Fremden auf der Tanzfläche ist. „Es ist keine Paarsache", betont er, diese „Vereinigung im Moment der geteilten Freude" – Blicke, Aufforderungen, Spiegelungen, seltsames Füreinander-Performen; spontan austesten, wie die Körper für die Dauer eines Liedes oder einer ganzen Nacht zusammenpassen könnten. Crimp glaubte, dass die *boogie intimacy* weit über das Angehen der Lichter hinausreichte; sie war ein radikaler Vorläufer der Schwulen- und Lesbenbewegung, „die Ausweitung von Möglichkeiten des Begehrens". Ich will den Spaß nicht aus dem Dancefloor heraustheoretisieren, als würde ich Schweiß aus einem trockenen Hemd auswringen wollen, aber mir ist bewusst, dass die Bereitschaft, sinnliche Zusammenkünfte zu entwerfen, eine Probe für andere gemeinsame Aktionen sein kann – für Solidarität und Experimente in unterschiedlichen Umgebungen.

d

Jimmy, Ain und Em erinnern sich an all die Clubs, in denen sie sich früher getroffen haben, und daran, wie durch die Inbesitznahme dieser Orte und deren Mitgestaltung ihre Freundschaft entstand. In diesem Gespräch schwingt eine gewisse Nostalgie mit, denn es findet in einer Zeit statt, in der es Lockdowns anstelle von Clubs gibt. Em beschreibt, wie die Organisation von Clubs als Startpunkt für die Entwicklung von größeren Hilfsstrukturen und die Mitwirkung in ihnen dienen kann: Beides hat die Eigenschaft, Verhältnisse zu bilden, aus denen physische und emotionale Räume für selbstorganisierte Aktionen hervorgehen können. Beides verweigert sich der Isolation. Em erwähnt einige Club-Crews, die sich in der Anfangsphase der Pandemie von laufenden Clubs in laufende Fürsorgegemeinschaften verwandelt haben.

Es ist jedoch nicht alles Utopie. Ethos und Ort befinden sich nicht immer im Einklang, und die Schlange vor einem Club hat ihre eigene Haltung. Jimmy spricht mit mir über den Türsteher als Grenzbereich zwischen verschiedenen Welten und unterschiedlichen Autoritäten. Die Sicherheit eines Gebäudes, einer Menschenmenge und wer jeweils hineingelassen wird, wer auf der Liste steht, warum wir die Dunkelheit überhaupt brauchen – das sind Fragen mit Antworten, die das Leben unterteilen und strukturieren, genau wie auch die Zugehörigkeiten.

Ich fühle mich an Ems Ausführungen darüber erinnert, was es bedeutet, durch Kunst einen sozialen Raum zu schaffen, und an die Weigerung, zwischen Autorschaft und Kollaboration zu unterscheiden: „Es gibt keine Notwendigkeit zu wissen, was genau wir tun werden, aber die Bereitwilligkeit,

es, wenn wir den Mut aufbringen, zuzulassen. In diesem Sinne könnte man sagen, dass dieses Denken dem anarchistischen oder nicht-autoritären sozialistischen Denken und Organisieren nahesteht. Es geht um die Neugier und Bereitschaft, Ressourcen und Wissen zu teilen und die Erfahrung der gemeinsamen Organisation zu machen, wobei der Prozess ebenso im Vordergrund steht wie das Endziel", sagt Em. „Kollaboration ist immer schon eine Abhängigkeit in Bezug auf soziale Beziehungen und Objekte oder Materialität, Technologien usw. Ich würde also nicht so sehr unterscheiden, ob ich kollaboriere oder nicht, sondern sagen, dass es immer schon eine Kollaboration ist, zu leben."

Im Sommer nach Jimmys Performance machen Em und ich eine Arbeitspause, um vor dem Büro eines Kunstmagazins zu protestieren, das eine öffentliche Podiumsdiskussion zum Thema „Cancel Culture" veranstaltet, dem Thema seiner neuesten Ausgabe. Die Diskussionsteilnehmer:innen scheinen sehr daran interessiert zu sein, ihren selbst erklärten Opferstatus in einem institutionellen Rahmen auszustellen, und der Verlag ist dazu bereit, zur Feier der neuen Ausgabe die Plattform dafür zu bieten. Ich frage mich, ob der Protest nur von uns beiden ausgehen wird. Auf jeden Fall bin ich bei meiner Ankunft überrascht, wie gut die Veranstaltung besucht ist und wie viele unserer Freund:innen und Kolleg:innen im Publikum sind. Ihr Erscheinen ist nicht spontan, sie haben sich im Voraus angemeldet.

Doch auch eine Reihe anderer Leute, die ich nicht kenne, sind wie wir unangekündigt zum Protest gekommen, und wir beginnen, eine Mahnwache

number of recent nightclub crews that, during the early part of the pandemic, transitioned from running clubs to running care communities.

It's not all utopia though. Ethos and place do not always congeal, and the line outside a club has its own attitude. Jimmy talks to me about the bouncer as the delineation between different worlds as well as different authorities. The safety of a building, of a crowd, and who is permitted into either, who gets to be on the list, why we need the dark in the first place – these are questions with answers that stratify and structure living as much as belonging.

I'm reminded of Em's account of what it means to create social space through art and their refusal to differentiate between authorship and collaboration: "There is no need to know what we will do but a willingness to let us do it if we dare. In this sense you could say it is close to anarchist or non-authoritative socialist thinking and organizing. It is a curiosity and a commitment to distributing resources and knowledge and having or making the experience of organizing and doing something collectively, with an emphasis on process as much as the final goal," they say. "Collaboration is already a dependency, with focus on the social relations and objects or materiality, technologies, etc. So I would not make so much of a distinction about whether I am collaborating or not, and say that it is always a collaboration, to live."

The summer after Jimmy's performance, Em and I take a break from work so we can stage an impromptu protest outside the offices of an art magazine holding a public panel on cancel culture, the theme of its latest edition. The panel seems keen to publicize their self-pronounced victimhood in an institutional space, and the publisher willing to provide that platform to celebrate the launch of its new issue. I wonder if the protest will just be the two of us. Certainly, on arrival, I am surprised at how well-attended the event is and how many friends and co-workers have turned up as audience. Their attendance isn't spontaneous; it's ticketed in advance.

But there are a number of other people who I don't know who have turned up, unprompted, in protest too, and we begin to form a picket. We each take turns speaking with the incoming audience, delaying them on the threshold of the steps between the street and the doors to the office, holding up the queue. We initiate conversations about why attendees want to be an audience to this discourse and whether different dialogues could be had instead and what their power is in this dynamic. We ask each other about different ways of assembling the kind of world we want. We ask for conversations about solidarity that might interrupt a discourse of scarcity and punishment. I notice our dialogues improve in depth and length as we work our way down the line of people, learning how to ask more precise questions, perhaps listen better, follow-up questions, and push back. We've all produced various printouts to distribute to the audience, with different links and information. Afterwards, Em and I go to the pub to decompress and read through the other protestors' texts.

Collaboration is about the space together, but Annie Dillard wants to talk about the space between.

zu bilden. Wir sprechen abwechselnd mit dem ankommenden Publikum, halten sie auf der Treppe zwischen der Straße und den Türen zum Büro auf und verzögern den Fortgang der Warteschlange. Wir beginnen Gespräche darüber, warum die Besucher:innen an diesem Diskurs teilnehmen wollen, ob man stattdessen andere Dialoge führen könnte und welche Machtposition sie in dieser Dynamik einnehmen. Wir stellen einander die Frage, welche Wege es gibt, die Welt so zu gestalten, wie wir sie uns wünschen. Wir fordern zu Gesprächsformen über Solidarität auf, die einen Diskurs über Mangel und Bestrafung unterbrechen könnten. Ich stelle fest, dass unsere Dialoge an Tiefe und Länge zunehmen, je weiter wir uns in der Reihe der Teilnehmenden nach hinten arbeiten und selber lernen, präzisere Fragen zu stellen, vielleicht besser zuzuhören, Fragen zu verfolgen und zu widersprechen. Wir haben diverse Printouts mit verschiedenen Links und Informationen zusammengestellt, die wir an die Anwesenden verteilen. Danach gehen Em und ich in eine Kneipe, um uns zu entspannen und die Texte der anderen Protestierenden durchzulesen.

Bei der Zusammenarbeit geht es um den gemeinsamen Raum, Annie Dillard aber möchte über den Raum dazwischen sprechen. Sie sagt, dass die Lücken das Entscheidende sind: „Go up into the gaps. If you can find them; they shift and vanish too. Stalk the gaps. Squeak into a gap in the soil, turn, and unlock – more than a maple – a universe. This is how you spend this afternoon, and tomorrow morning, and tomorrow afternoon. Spend the afternoon. You can't take it with you".*

Ich frage mich, wie die Lücken klingen und wie man auf sie achten kann: die Schwelle zwischen dem, was wir denken, und dem, was wir sagen; das unbeholfene Stocken oder das unerträgliche Warten zwischen dem Ruf und der Antwort; das Hervorspringen der Geschichten, die wir einander erzählen, und ihr Zögern, das, was wir aus Angst vor Hässlichkeit und Zurückweisung weglassen. Manchmal brauche ich andere Menschen, die mich auf die Lücken hinweisen, die mir zeigen, wie diese stillen Bereiche die lauteren Teile strukturieren.

* „Geh rein in die Lücken. Wenn du sie finden kannst; sie verschieben sich und verschwinden. Verfolge die Lücken. Krieche in eine Lücke in der Erde, drehe dich um und brich auf – wie ein Ahorn, wie das Universum. Verbring so den heutigen Nachmittag, den nächsten Morgen, den nächsten Nachmittag. Nutze den Nachmittag. Du kannst ihn nicht mitnehmen."

She says that the gaps are the thing: "Go up into
the gaps. If you can find them; they shift and vanish
too. Stalk the gaps. Squeak into a gap in the soil,
turn, and unlock – more than a maple – a universe.
This is how you spend this afternoon, and tomorrow
morning, and tomorrow afternoon. Spend the
afternoon. You can't take it with you."

I wonder what the gaps sound like and how to
listen out for them: the threshold between what
we think and what we say; the awkward hesitations
or unbearable waiting between the call and the
response; the leaping and the lingering of the
stories we tell each other, what we skim off for
fear of ugliness and rejection. Sometimes I need
other people to point the gaps out, to show me
how these quiet spaces structure the louder parts.